Also by Marie A. DiCowden, Ph.D., SFNAP
a.k.a. *Heart*

The Colors of Prayer

Balboa Press books may be ordered through booksellers or by contacting:

Balboa Press
A Division of Hay House
1663 Liberty Drive
Bloomington, IN 47403
www.balboapress.com
844-682-1282

ISBN: 978-1-9822-7290-6 (sc)
ISBN: 978-1-9822-7291-3 (e)

Print information available on the last page.

Balboa Press rev. date: 11/05/2021

BALBOA.PRESS
A DIVISION OF HAY HOUSE

BiBi and Alfie: BFF -

A Story of True Friendship

Marie A. DiCowden, Ph.D., SFNAP

This book is based on the true story and true friendship of BiBi, the Pug, and Alfie, the Maltese. It is dedicated to their memory and to the memory of Mama Pearl.

GROWING UP IN FLORIDA

This is the story of BiBi and Alfie. A story of best friends forever--BFF. A true friendship. BiBi was a Chinese Pug that lived across the hall from Alfie, a Maltese. They met when they were both little puppies and grew up together.

BiBi lived in an apartment in Florida with her mother, Mommy M and Alfie lived in the apartment across the hall with his mother, Mama Pearl. As puppies they played together at each other's homes. In fact, they spent as much time at each other's home as they did at their own. It was actually like they had two apartments of their own and allowed their Mamas to live with them! They played in each other's apartment, ate in each other's apartment, and sometimes took naps in each other's apartment!

Another fun place to play was in the long hallway. They would find a ball or a toy and run up and down the hallway chasing each other.

Sometimes they would even take both ends of a toy in their mouths at the same time and, between them with each holding on to one end, Alfie and BiBi would run up and down the hall together.

They played together, walked together, ate together, snacked together, slept together.

They even went together to see Dr. John, their veterinarian together! He kept them strong and healthy.

Everybody knew that BiBi and Alfie were a couple!

ALFIE AND MAMA PEARL

Alfie was a Mama's boy. He loved his best friend, BiBi, so much. But the only one he loved even more was his Mama Pearl.

Alfie would go to bed every night at 9:00 o'clock. Even if BiBi and Mommy M were visiting with him and Mama Pearl. At 9:00 pm sharp, he would crawl into one of his beds that Mama Pearl kept in the kitchen. BiBi and Mommy M and Mama Pearl would stay up and talk and laugh and bark while Alfie slept! Sometimes Mama Pearl would call him "The Old Man" because he had to go to bed right at 9:00 pm every night!

BiBi liked her sleep too. But she preferred to sleep late in the morning. She was a sweet and spoiled little puggie! Sometimes she would not get up until 1:00 pm in the afternoon. And that was just fine with Mommy M. BiBi, Mommy M and Mama Pearl all enjoyed their night activities. They were nocturnal creatures. So, sleeping late was fun for them too! BiBi liked to sleep on her back. BiBi would dream. Sometimes she would bark in her sleep. But she always dreamt of Alfie!

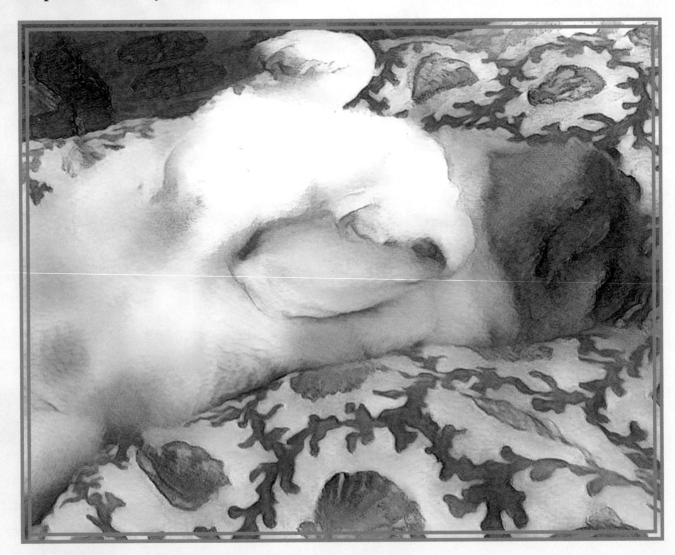

BIBI AND MOMMY M

BiBi was devoted to her Mommy too! She and Mommy M were always having fun. BiBi even went to work with her Mommy M and made many friends. They had parties whenever they could. They especially loved Halloween and would always dress up!

BIBI AND ALFIE TRAVEL TO VIRGINIA

Mommy M and BiBi also traveled together a lot. One favorite place to visit was the old family house in Virginia. It had been built in 1830 and had lots of fun places to hide and play.

One time, Alfie and Mama Pearl traveled to Virginia with Mommy M and BiBi. They flew on a big plane and were quite well behaved! There was an empty seat between Mommy M and Mama Pearl where BiBi and Alfie got to sit.

When the snacks came around, BiBi and Alfie were served their own water and allowed to eat snacks on their own tray! Of course, they played and ate and walked and slept together at BiBi's Virginia home just like they did in their apartments at their Florida home!

ALFIE AND BIBI – BFF EVERYWHERE!

Alfie was a handsome guy. There were other doggies in his extended family, and he had other doggie friends, but it was clear that his best friend in the whole world was BiBi. BiBi was a beautiful fawn pug who loved everyone but was closest to her best friend, Alfie.

While BiBi and Alfie walked together a lot, one thing that they did NOT like to do was to walk in the rain! But sometimes, despite the weather, Mama Pearl and Mommy M had to walk them and each went with their own mother. Alfie would just run in and out very fast if Mama Pearl took him out in the rain.

BiBi had to be coaxed and carried and given treats to get her to go out in the rain at all! One time Mommy M even bought BiBi a special raincoat so she wouldn't get wet. But BiBi was not too impressed and rarely wore it.

BIBI AND ALFIE PLAY DATES—DRESS UP AND OTHER THINGS

Alfie and BiBi liked dressing up together. Sometimes when it was cold, they put on their sweaters. Once a friend in Taiwan sent BiBi some Chinese outfits so she could be a real Chinese pug....like her ancestors!

The outfits were made of beautiful satin. One was ruby red, and the other was royal blue. They each had beautiful Chinese embroidery too! BiBi shared her Chinese clothes with Alfie since he was her best friend. So, Alfie got to dress up too. Even though he was Maltese! They would parade around in their clothes for a while before they got too tired and just stripped down to their fur!

Alfie and BiBi were such close friends that each knew when the other was home. Sometimes if they wanted to visit, one would go to the door in their apartment and ask their Mama to let them out. Then they would go across the hall and sit outside the other one's door. Because they were so close the one that was inside would bark to let the other mother know it was time to open the door and let their best friend in! But the doggie waiting outside the door never had to bark a word!

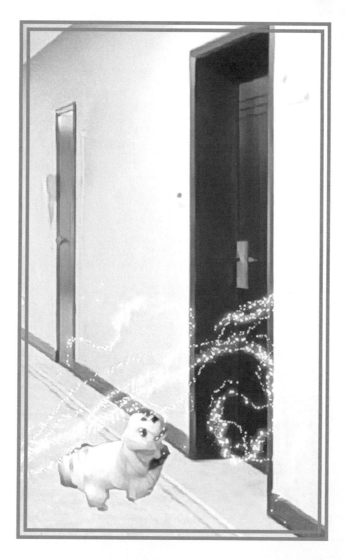

They also had special play times every week that BiBi and Alfie set for themselves. Every Saturday afternoon was a play date. And every Sunday evening BiBi insisted on eating at Alfie's house. BiBi would refuse to eat her own dinner at home on Sunday. She preferred to eat with Alfie. If Mama Pearl made something special for Alfie, BiBi had to have it too. Or even if there wasn't any special dinner, BiBi would insist that her plate be taken to Alfie's house so she could eat with him.

One Saturday afternoon, Mama Pearl had to take Alfie with her and go out for a long afternoon of shopping. The shopping went past the time for Alfie and BiBi's regular play time together.

BiBi kept wanting to look out the door and go see Alfie, but Mommy M had to tell her that Alfie was not home.

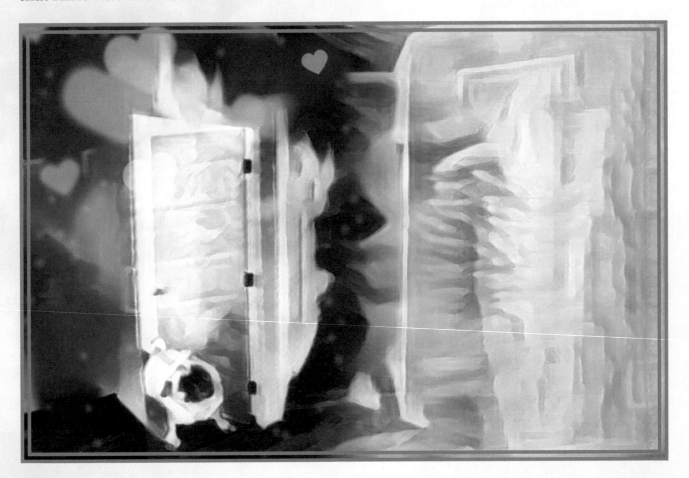

Mommy M would open the door and BiBi would look out in the hall and see.... No Alfie! So, she would hang her head and come back inside.

Then late in the afternoon, BiBi insisted on having the door opened for the fifth time. Mommy M told BiBi, "Alfie is not there. You will see." As soon as Mommy M opened the door, she looked down the hall. The elevator doors opened and there was Alfie with Mama Pearl! It was like BiBi and Alfie had built-in radar for each other. It was the Magic of True Friendship!

WALKING MY BIBI BACK HOME

BiBi hated to see Alfie leave when it was time to go home. And the same was true of Alfie. He hated to see BiBi leave too! When Alfie would head out the door, BiBi would go out also and walk with him to his door. Then when BiBi would leave to walk back to her door, Alfie would walk back with BiBi. And then it started all over! Back and forth and back and forth. Sometimes it would take 10 minutes to walk each other across the hall to each other's door before their Mommies made them say good night!

MARIE A. DICOWDEN

BIBI AND ALFIE ENJOY THE SEASON OF LIGHTS: HANUKKAH AND CHRISTMAS

Christmas and Hanukkah holidays were always a special time for Alfie and BiBi. Mommy M had a big dinner at her place. The grandchildren and their parents would come and so would Mama Pearl and Alfie. BiBi and Alfie always exchanged gifts.

One time Alfie actually gave BiBi a Cinderella shoe! It was plush and soft and just made to chew on. It squeaked too!

Of course, BiBi and Alfie played with the children, played with the wrapping paper and ribbon...

...and ate holiday food just like their humans. (But only the food that Dr. John said they could have " just a little" for a treat.)

That was one night that Alfie always stayed up past 9:00 o'clock! And he didn't even seem to seem to mind one bit!

ALFIE AND BIBI AT THE RAINBOW BRIDGE

BiBi and Alfie were best friends for 11 years. Alfie and BiBi shared true love and loyalty. They were soulmates! BiBi and Alfie showed us what true friends really are. Now they run and play together across the Rainbow Bridge. We miss them so much. But their lives gave us memories too beautiful to forget!

...you lived and your lives gave us memories too beautiful to forget!

With Thanks

Thanks to so many people who participated in the lives and friendship of BiBi and Alfie... Eleanor, Lynn, Rosa, the Rosenberg and Cowden/DiCowden families, all the people at Biscayne Institutes, the neighbors and friends at Portsview and Honeycomb House and, of course, to Dr. John Eccer at Just Paws veterinarians in Pembroke Pines! And a special special thanks to the original Biscayne Bubbles, the First Pug of Them All. Bubbles you were here way too short a time, but it is you who opened our hearts to the deep friendship for all the pugs to come and all their friends who followed them into our hearts and lives.

Biscayne Bubbles, The First Pug of Them All

Printed in the United States
by Baker & Taylor Publisher Services